KT-551-183

M^{RS} BEETON'S
HOME COOKING

SOUPS

WARD LOCK LIMITED · LONDON

© Ward Lock Limited 1986

First published in Great Britain
in 1986 by Ward Lock Limited,
82 Gower Street,
London W1X 1RB,
an Egmont Company.

Edited by Susan Dixon
Designed by Melissa Orrom
Text filmset in Caslon 540
by Cheney & Sons Limited
Printed and bound in Italy by
L.E.G.O.

**British Library Cataloguing in
Publication Data**

Soups.—
(Mrs. Beeton's home cooking)
  1. Soups
  I. Series
  641.8′13   TX757

ISBN 0-7063-6454-6

Notes
The recipes in this book have
been tested in metric weights
and measures. These have
been based on equivalents of
25g to 1 oz, 500g to 1 lb and
500ml to 1 pint, with some
adjustments where necessary.

It is important to follow *either*
the metric *or* the imperial
measures. Do not use a
combination of measures.

SOUPS

The principal art in composing good rich soup, is so to proportion the several ingredients that the flavour of one shall not predominate over another, and that all the articles of which it is composed, shall form an agreeable whole. To accomplish this, care must be taken that the roots and herbs are perfectly well cleaned, and that the water is proportioned to the quantity of meat and other ingredients.

Isabella Beeton 1861

On pages 2 and 3
From the left, clockwise
Hollandaise Soup (page 48), Spring Broth (page 16) and
Jellied Tomato Soup with Soured Cream (page 60)

STOCKS

BROWN STOCK

(Beef stock)

Makes 1.5 litres/3 pints (approx)

500g/1 lb beef *or* veal marrow
  bones
500g/1 lb lean shin of beef
1.5 litres/3 pints cold water
1 × 5ml spoon/1 teaspoon salt
1 medium-sized onion

1 medium-sized carrot
1 stick of celery
bouquet garni
1 × 2.5ml spoon/½ teaspoon black
  peppercorns

Ask the butcher to chop the bones into manageable pieces. Wipe them thoroughly. Trim off any fat and cut the meat into small pieces. Put the bones and meat in a roasting tin in a hot oven at 220°C/425°F/Gas 7, for 30-40 minutes to brown, turning them occasionally.

Put the browned bones and meat in a large saucepan with the water and salt. Prepare and slice the vegetables. Add them to the pan with the bouquet garni and peppercorns. Heat slowly to boiling point, skim well, and cover the pan with a tight-fitting lid. Reduce the heat and simmer very gently for 4 hours. Strain through a fine sieve and leave to cool. When cold, remove any fat from the surface.

Brown Stock

GENERAL HOUSEHOLD STOCK

Makes 1 litre/2 pints (approx)

1kg/2 lb cooked *or* raw bones of any
  meat *or* poultry, cooked *or* raw
  meat trimmings, giblets, and
  bacon rinds
500g/1 lb onions, carrots, celery,
  and leeks

salt
1 bay leaf
4 black peppercorns

Break or chop the bones into manageable pieces. Wipe thoroughly. Prepare and slice the vegetables, retaining a piece of brown onion skin if a brown stock is required. Put the bones and meat trimmings into a saucepan. Cover with cold water and add 1 × 2.5ml spoon/½ teaspoon salt for each litre/2 pints of water used. Heat slowly to simmering point. Add the other ingredients. Simmer, uncovered, for at least 3 hours. Strain and cool quickly by standing the pan in chilled water. When cold, skim off the fat. If the stock is not required at once, keep it cold. Use within 24 hours, or within 3 days if kept in a refrigerator. Reboil before use.

WHITE STOCK

Makes 2 litres/4 pints (approx)

1kg/2 lb knuckle of veal
1 medium-sized onion
1 stick of celery
2 litres/4 pints cold water
1 × 10ml spoon/1 dessertspoon salt

1 × 10ml spoon/1 dessertspoon
    white vinegar *or* lemon juice
1 × 2.5ml spoon/½ teaspoon white
    peppercorns
a small strip of lemon rind
1 bay leaf

Chop the knuckle into manageable pieces. Scrape the bones, trim off any fat, and wipe the bones thoroughly. Prepare and slice the onion and celery. Put the bones in a large pan with the cold water, salt, and vinegar or lemon juice. Heat to boiling point and skim. Add the vegetables and the other ingredients. Bring back to the boil, cover, reduce the heat, and simmer gently for 4 hours. Strain the stock through a fine sieve and cool it quickly by standing the pan in chilled water. When cold, skim off the fat. Store as for General Household Stock (page 8).

STEWPAN.

CHICKEN STOCK

Makes 1 litre/2 pints (using 1 litre/2 pints water)

1 medium-sized onion
1 stick of celery
carcass of 1 chicken *or* game bird,
  including the giblets

cleaned feet of bird (optional)
1 × 10ml spoon/1 dessertspoon salt
4 white peppercorns
bouquet garni

Prepare and slice the vegetables. Break or chop the carcass into manageable pieces. Put the carcass, giblets, and feet, if used, in a large saucepan, cover with cold water, and add the salt. Heat to boiling point. Draw the pan off the heat and leave to stand for 2–3 minutes, then skim off any fat. Add the vegetables, peppercorns, and bouquet garni. Re-heat to boiling point, cover, reduce the heat, and simmer very gently for 3–4 hours. Strain the stock through a fine sieve and cool it quickly by standing the container in chilled water. When cold, skim off the fat. Store as for General Household Stock (page 8).

FISH STOCK

Makes 1 litre/2 pints (using 1 litre/2 pints water)

bones, skin, and heads from
    filleted fish *or* fish trimmings *or*
    cod's *or* other fish heads *or* any
    mixture of these
1 × 5ml spoon/1 teaspoon salt

1 small onion
1 stick of celery
4 white peppercorns
bouquet garni

Break up the bones and wash the fish trimmings, if used. Prepare
and slice the vegetables. Put the bones, fish trimmings, or heads in
a saucepan and cover with cold water. Add the salt. Heat to boiling
point. Add the vegetables, the peppercorns, and bouquet garni.
Cover, and simmer gently for 40 minutes. Strain the stock through
a fine sieve.

Note If cooked for longer than 40 minutes, fish stock tastes bitter.
It does not keep unless frozen, and should be made only as
required.

COURT BOUILLON

(for salmon, salmon trout, and other whole fish)

water
500ml/1 pint dry white wine *or* dry
    cider to each litre/2 pints water
2 × 15ml spoons/2 tablespoons
    white wine vinegar to each litre/2
    pints water
2 large carrots

2 large onions
2–3 sticks celery
parsley stalks
1 bouquet garni to each litre/2 pints
    water
a few peppercorns
salt and pepper

Put the liquids in a large pan. Slice the carrots and onions, chop the
celery, and crush the parsley stalks. Add to the liquid with the
remaining ingredients. Simmer for 30 minutes, leave to cool, then
strain and use as required.

VEGETABLE STOCK

Makes 2 litres/4 pints (approx)

2 large carrots
2 medium-sized onions
3 sticks celery
2 tomatoes
25g/1oz butter *or* margarine
2 litres/4 pints boiling water

1 × 2.5ml spoon/½ teaspoon yeast
  extract
bouquet garni
1 × 5ml spoon/1 teaspoon salt
6 black peppercorns
a blade of mace
outer leaves of 1 lettuce *or* ¼ small
  cabbage

Slice the carrots, onions, and celery thinly and chop the tomatoes. Melt the fat in a large saucepan and fry the carrots, onions, and celery for 5–10 minutes until the onions are golden-brown. Add the tomatoes and fry for a further minute. Add the water and the rest of the ingredients, except the lettuce or cabbage. Cover, and simmer for 1 hour. Shred the lettuce or cabbage, and add to the pan. Simmer for a further 20 minutes. Strain through a fine sieve. Use the same day, if possible, or cool quickly and store in a refrigerator for up to 2 days.

CARROTS.

THIN SOUPS & CONSOMMÉS

CHICKEN BROTH

8 helpings

1 small boiling fowl (1.5kg/3 lb approx) *or* 1 chicken carcass with some flesh left on it
giblets of the bird
1.5–2 litres/3–4 pints water
1 × 5ml spoon/1 teaspoon salt
1 medium-sized onion
2 medium-sized carrots
1 stick of celery
½ × 2.5ml spoon/¼ teaspoon ground pepper
a blade of mace
bouquet garni
a strip of lemon rind
25g/1oz long-grain rice (optional)
1 × 15ml spoon/1 tablespoon chopped parsley

Joint the boiling fowl or break up the carcass bones, and wash the giblets. Put them into a large saucepan and cover with the cold water. Add the salt, and heat slowly to simmering point. Cut the onion in half, and dice the carrots and celery. Add the vegetables to the pan with the pepper, mace, bouquet garni, and lemon rind. Cover, and simmer gently for 3–3½ hours if using a raw boiling fowl, or for 1½ hours if using a chicken carcass. Strain the broth through a colander. Skim off the fat.

Return the broth to the pan and re-heat to simmering point. Wash the rice, if used, and sprinkle it into the broth. Cover, and simmer for a further 15–20 minutes until the rice is cooked.

Some of the meat can be chopped finely and added to the broth, the rest can be used in made-up dishes, eg a fricassée. Just before serving the broth, re-season if required, and add the chopped parsley.

Chicken Broth

SPRING BROTH

12 spring onions
4 young carrots
1 small turnip
a few heads sprue asparagus
100g/4oz shelled green peas
2 × 10ml spoons/2 dessertspoons
  olive oil *or* butter

1 litre/2 pints white stock (page 9)
  or general household stock (page
  8)
salt and pepper
1 × 10ml spoon/1 dessertspoon
  chopped parsley

Cut the spring onions and carrots into thin rings and the turnip into
6mm/¼ inch dice. Remove the tips of the asparagus and reserve.
Cut the tender parts of the stalks into 6mm/¼ inch lengths. Heat
the oil or butter in a pan, add all the vegetables, cover, and cook
over gentle heat for about 10 minutes. Do not let them brown.
Heat the stock to boiling point, add to the pan, cover, and simmer
gently for 30 minutes. Add the asparagus tips, cover, and simmer
for a further 15 minutes. Season to taste, and add the chopped
parsley just before serving.

SCOTS OR SCOTCH BROTH

4–6 helpings

500g/1lb scrag end of neck of
    mutton
1 × 5ml spoon/1 teaspoon salt
1 litre/2 pints cold water
50g/2oz pearl barley
2 medium carrots

2 leeks
1 small turnip
1 stick of celery
pepper
1 × 10ml spoon/1 dessertspoon
    chopped parsley

Wipe and trim the meat, and cut into 2.5cm/1 inch pieces. Put into
a deep pan with the bones, salt, and cold water. Heat gently to
simmering point. Blanch the barley. Add to the pan, cover and
simmer gently for 2 hours. Prepare the vegetables, setting aside
one whole carrot and cutting the rest into 6mm/¼ inch dice. Add
them to the broth, cover, and simmer for another hour. Grate the
whole carrot and add it to the broth 20 minutes before serving.
Skim the fat. Remove the bones. Season to taste with pepper and
add the chopped parsley just before serving.

Overleaf
From the top, clockwise
Green Herb Consommé (page 24), *Scots Broth (above)* and
Consommé Brunoise (page 21)

HOTCH POTCH

8 helpings

1kg/2lb scrag and middle neck of
   lamb *or* mutton
1.25 litres/2½ pints water
1 × 10ml spoon/1 dessertspoon salt
bouquet garni
1 medium-sized carrot
1 small turnip
6 spring onions

1 small lettuce
100g/4oz shelled young broad
   beans *or* runner beans
100g/4oz cauliflower florets
150g/5oz shelled peas
salt and pepper
1 × 15ml spoon/1 tablespoon
   chopped parsley

Wipe the meat and trim off any excess fat. Remove the meat from
the bone and cut the meat into small pieces. Put the bone and
meat into a large saucepan, add the water, and heat very slowly to
simmering point. Add the salt and the bouquet garni, cover, and
simmer very gently for 30 minutes.

   Meanwhile, cut the carrot and turnip into 6mm/¼ inch dice and
the spring onions into thin rings; shred the lettuce and runner
beans, if used. Add the carrot, turnip, and spring onions to the
pan, cover, and simmer for 1½ hours. Add the rest of the
vegetables to the soup, cover, and simmer for a further 30 minutes.
Season to taste. Skim off the fat and remove the bouquet garni and
the bones. Add the chopped parsley just before serving.

Note The vegetables can be varied according to the season.

CONSOMMÉ BRUNOISE

1 × 2.5ml spoon/½ teaspoon
  lemon juice
1 × 15ml spoon/1 tablespoon
  sherry (optional)
1 × 15ml spoon/1 tablespoon finely
  diced carrot

1 × 15ml spoon/1 tablespoon finely
  diced turnip
1 × 15ml spoon/1 tablespoon finely
  diced greek leek
1 × 15ml spoon/1 tablespoon finely
  diced celery

CONSOMMÉ

100g/4oz lean shin of beef
125ml/¼ pint water
1 small onion
1 small carrot
1 small stick of celery

1.25 litres/2½ pints cold brown
  stock (page 6)
bouquet garni
½ × 2.5ml spoon/¼ teaspoon salt
4 white peppercorns
white and crushed shell of 1 egg

Make the consommé first. Shred the beef finely, trimming off all
the fat. Soak the meat in the water for 15 minutes. Prepare the
vegetables. Put the meat, water, and the rest of the ingredients
into a deep saucepan adding the egg white and shell last. Heat
slowly to simmering point, whisking all the time, until a froth rises
to the surface. Remove the whisk, cover, and simmer the
consommé very gently for 1½–2 hours. Do not allow to boil or the
froth will break up and cloud the consommé. Strain slowly into a
basin through muslin or a scalded jelly bag. If necessary, strain the
consommé again.

Re-heat the consommé to boiling point, and add the lemon juice
and sherry, if used. Cook the diced vegetables very carefully in
boiling salted water until just tender. Drain and rinse the
vegetables; then put them into a warmed tureen.

Pour the hot consommé over the diced vegetables, and serve.

Note This recipe makes 1 litre/2 pints consommé.

CLEAR TOMATO SOUP

4–6 helpings

2 medium-sized tomatoes

1 litre/2 pints consommé (page 21)
white and crushed shell of 1 egg

GARNISH (optional)

orange *or* lemon slices

1 × 15ml spoon/1 tablespoon each
of diced carrot, celery, and green
leek

Skin the tomatoes and cut them into small pieces. Add to the consommé, heat to simmering point, and simmer for 10 minutes. Strain the consommé, then return it to the pan. Add the egg white and shell, re-heat slowly to simmering point, whisking all the time, until a froth rises to the surface. Strain slowly into a basin through muslin or a scalded jelly bag; if necessary, strain again.

Garnish, if liked, with orange or lemon slices. Alternatively, cook the diced vegetables separately in boiling salted water until tender. Drain and put in a warmed tureen. Re-heat the consommé and pour over them.

Clear Tomato Soup

Green Herb Consommé

2 medium-sized tomatoes
1 litre/2 pints white stock (page 9)
    or chicken stock (page 10)
a bunch of fresh mixed herbs
    (marjoram, basil, thyme)

white and crushed shell of 1 egg
1 × 2.5ml spoon/½ teaspoon
    lemon juice
50ml/2 fl oz dry white wine
    (optional)

GARNISH

1 × 15ml spoon/1 tablespoon
    shredded lettuce leaves
1 × 15ml spoon/1 tablespoon
    shredded spinach *or* sorrel leaves
1 × 15ml spoon/1 tablespoon small
    green peas

1 × 10ml spoon/1 dessertspoon
    shredded cucumber rind
extra white stock
6 mint leaves
6 chives
6 chervil leaves

Skin the tomatoes and dice the flesh. Heat the stock to boiling point and add the tomatoes and herbs. Add the white and shell and heat slowly to simmering point, whisking all the time, until a froth rises to the surface. Remove the whisk, cover, and simmer very gently for 30 minutes only. Strain slowly into a basin through muslin or a scalded jelly bag.

Meanwhile, cook the vegetables for the garnish separately in a little boiling stock until just tender. Chop the mint and the chives.

Heat the consommé to boiling point and add the cooked vegetables for the garnish with the stock in which they were cooked. Re-heat for 1 minute only. Just before serving, add the lemon juice, wine, if used, and chopped mint and chives. Float 1 chervil leaf on top of each helping.

THICK SOUPS

CREAM OF CHICKEN SOUP

—— 4–6 helpings ——

25g/1oz cornflour
125ml/¼ pint milk
1 litre/2 pints chicken stock (page 10)
50g/2oz cooked chicken
salt and pepper

1 × 5ml spoon/1 teaspoon lemon juice
a pinch of grated nutmeg
2 egg yolks
2 × 15ml spoons/2 tablespoons single cream

Blend the cornflour with a little of the milk. Heat the stock to boiling point and stir into the blended cornflour. Return the mixture to the pan and re-heat to boiling point, stirring all the time. Reduce the heat, cover, and simmer for 20 minutes. Cut the chicken into 6mm/¼ inch dice and heat these in the soup. Season to taste, and add the lemon juice and nutmeg. Beat the yolks with the rest of the milk and the cream; beat in a little hot soup, and fold into the rest of the soup. Heat until it thickens, but do not allow it to boil.

THE NUTMEG.

COCK-A-LEEKIE

100g/4oz prunes
1 small boiling fowl with giblets
  (1.5kg/3lb approx)
3 rashers streaky bacon, without
  rinds (optional)
1kg/2lb veal *or* beef marrow bones
  (optional)

500g/1lb leeks
1.5–2 litres/3–4 pints cold water
2 × 5ml spoons/2 teaspoons salt
½ × 2.5ml spoon/¼ teaspoon
  pepper
bouquet garni

Soak the prunes overnight in cold water; then stone them. Wipe
the fowl and wash the giblets. Chop the bacon, if used. Chop the
bones into manageable pieces, if used. Wash and trim the leeks
and cut them into thin rings. Put the fowl, giblets, marrow bones,
and bacon into a deep pan, cover with cold water, add the salt, and
heat very slowly to simmering point. Reserve 4 × 15ml spoons/4
tablespoons of the leeks and add the remaining leeks, the pepper,
and bouquet garni to the pan. Cover, and simmer gently for about
3 hours, or until the fowl is tender.

   Remove the fowl, carve off the meat and cut it into fairly large
serving pieces. Strain the liquid. Return the pieces to the soup
with the soaked and stoned prunes and the remaining sliced leeks.
Simmer very gently for 30 minutes until the prunes are just tender
but not broken. Re-season if required, and serve the soup with the
prunes.

BROWN WINDSOR SOUP

— *6 helpings* —

150g/5oz shin of beef
150g/5oz stewing lamb
1 medium-sized onion
1 carrot
35g/1½oz butter
35g/1½oz flour
1.75 litres/3½ pints beef stock *or*
  strong general household stock
  (page 8)

bouquet garni
salt
a few grains Cayenne pepper
75ml/3fl oz brown sherry *or*
  Madeira (optional)
35g/1½oz boiled rice (optional)

GARNISH
toasted croûtons

Cut the beef and lamb into 2.5cm/1 inch pieces. Skin and slice the onion, and slice the carrot. Heat the butter in a deep heavy saucepan, put in the meat and vegetables, and fry gently until lightly browned. Stir in the flour, and continue cooking until it is well browned. Add the stock gradually, stirring all the time. Heat to boiling point, add the bouquet garni, cover, reduce the heat, and simmer for 2 hours or until the meat is very tender. Season to taste with salt and Cayenne pepper.

Strain the soup into a clean pan. Discard the bouquet garni, and remove any bones, skin and gristle from the meat. Return the meat to the soup, and either rub through a sieve or process in an electric blender to obtain a smooth purée. Return the purée to the pan, add the sherry or Madeira if used, and re-season if required. Just before serving, add the rice if used, and re-heat throroughly. Serve garnished with croûtons.

MULLIGATAWNY SOUP

400g/13oz lean mutton, rabbit,
    stewing veal *or* shin of beef
1 medium-sized onion
1 small cooking apple
25g/1oz butter *or* margarine
2 × 15ml spoons/2 tablespoons
    curry powder
25g/1oz plain flour
1 litre/2 pints water

1 large carrot
½ small parsnip
bouquet garni
1 × 2.5ml spoon/½ teaspoon
    lemon juice
1 × 2.5ml spoon/½ teaspoon salt
½ × 2.5ml spoon/¼ teaspoon
    black treacle *or* extra lemon juice

Trim off any fat and cut the meat into small pieces. Prepare the onion and apple and chop them finely. Melt the fat in a deep saucepan and fry the onion and apple quickly for 2–3 minutes. Add the curry powder, cook gently for 2 minutes, then stir in the flour. Gradually add the water and stir until boiling. Add the meat. Prepare and slice the carrot and parsnip, and add to the pan with the bouquet garni, lemon juice, and salt. Simmer until the meat is very tender. This will take 2 hours for rabbit, 3 hours for stewing veal and mutton, and 4 hours for shin of beef.

Taste the soup, and add black treacle or more lemon juice to obtain a flavour that is neither predominantly sweet nor acid. Strain the soup. Dice some of the meat finely, add to the soup and re-heat.

Serve with boiled long-grain rice.

Note The amount of curry powder can be varied to taste; the quantity given above is for a mild-flavoured soup.

OXTAIL SOUP

4–6 helpings

1 oxtail
25g/1oz beef dripping
1 medium-sized onion
1 large carrot
1 turnip
1 stick of celery

1 litre/2 pints water *or* general
  household stock (page 8)
1 × 5ml spoon/1 teaspoon salt
bouquet garni
6 black peppercorns
25g/1oz plain flour

Wash, trim off any fat, and joint the tail. Heat the dripping in a saucepan. Add half the jointed tail and fry until the meat is browned. Lift out the meat and reserve the fat in the pan. Prepare and slice the vegetables. Fry in the hot dripping until golden-brown, then remove. Put all the oxtail and the fried vegetables into a deep saucepan. Add the water or stock, and heat very slowly to boiling point. Add the salt, bouquet garni, and peppercorns. Cover, and simmer very gently for 3–4 hours.

Meanwhile, stir the flour into the dripping in the saucepan and fry gently until golden-brown. Strain the soup. Remove all the meat from the bones. Return some of the smaller pieces of meat and any small slices of carrot to the soup. Whisk in the browned flour. Re-heat the soup to boiling point, whisking all the time. Re-season if required.

Oxtail Soup

FISHERMAN'S HOT POT

50g/2oz white cabbage
100g/4oz leek
250g/8oz potatoes
100g/4oz onions
25g/1oz red pepper
2 slices white bread
50ml/2fl oz cooking oil
25g/1oz butter
250g/8oz cod *or* other white fish
 fillets (see **Note**)

150ml/6fl oz Muscadet *or* other dry
 white wine
1 litre/2 pints water
50g/2oz concentrated tomato purée
1 chicken stock cube
bouquet garni
1 clove of garlic
salt and pepper

GARNISH

1 × 15ml spoon/1 tablespoon
 chopped parsley

Shred the cabbage, slice the leek and potatoes, chop the onion and pepper. Remove the crusts from the bread, cut into 1.25cm/½ inch cubes, and dry in the oven for 10 minutes.

Heat the oil and butter in a large saucepan, add the vegetables, cover, and cook gently for 7–8 minutes; do not let them colour. Skin the fish, cut them into 2.5cm/1 inch cubes, and fry for 3 minutes with the vegetables, turning them over to firm the surface of the cubes. Pour in the wine, water, and tomato purée. Crumble in the stock cube. Skin and crush the garlic. Add the bouquet garni and garlic, and season to taste. Heat to simmering point and simmer for 20 minutes. Discard the bouquet garni. Pour into a soup tureen and sprinkle with the chopped parsley.

Note Any white fish can be used for the hot pot, eg haddock, hake, whiting, ling, etc.

HADDOCK, COD OR SKATE SOUP

625g/1¼lb haddock, cod, skate *or* any available white fish
2 large onions
1 large carrot
2 sticks celery
200g/7oz potatoes
25g/1oz butter
2 × 10ml spoons/2 dessertspoons olive oil
1 × 5ml spoon/1 teaspoon curry powder
750ml/1½ pints boiling water
bouquet garni
salt and pepper
50ml/2fl oz white wine (optional)
25g/1oz flour
125ml/¼ pint milk
75ml/3fl oz single cream

Prepare the fish and cut them into small pieces. Prepare the onions, carrot, and celery and slice thinly. Peel and dice the potatoes. Heat the butter and olive oil in a deep saucepan. Add all the vegetables and fry gently for 10 minutes. Stir in the curry powder and cook for 3 minutes. Add the boiling water, bouquet garni, and seasoning to taste. Add the fish and re-heat the soup to simmering point; cover, and simmer until the fish is tender.

Transfer the best pieces of fish from the soup and keep them hot in a little of the liquid. Simmer the rest of the soup, uncovered, for 15 minutes until it is reduced. Remove the bouquet garni and rub the soup through a sieve, or process in an electric blender. Add the wine, if used, and re-heat the soup. Blend the flour with a little of the cold milk and then stir in the rest of the milk. Stir it into the soup and heat to boiling point. Add the pieces of fish and the cream to the soup at boiling point, but do not reboil.

WHITE FISH CHOWDER

125ml/¼ pint dry white wine
1 litre/2 pints water
bouquet garni
salt and pepper
400g/13oz skinned coley fillets *or*
  other coarse-fleshed white fish

75g/3oz leek
75g/3oz carrot
50g/2oz butter
50g/2oz flour
1 × 5ml spoon/1 teaspoon turmeric
3 × 15ml spoon/3 tablespoons
  chopped parsley

Put the wine, water, bouquet garni, and seasoning in a pan and poach the fish gently in the liquid until tender. Meanwhile, prepare and dice the leek and carrot. Strain the soup into a clean pan. Remove the bouquet garni and cut the fish into 1.25cm/½ inch cubes. Return the pan to the heat and heat to simmering point. Cream the butter and flour to a smooth paste, then add it gradually to the soup, whisking in each addition. Stir in the turmeric. Add the diced vegetables and simmer gently for 7 minutes. Add the fish and the parsley. Simmer for a further 5 minutes.

Serve hot with crusty bread.

White Fish Chowder

LOBSTER BISQUE

4–6 helpings

shell, trimmings, and a little of the flesh of a small *or* medium-sized lobster
1 medium-sized onion
1 medium-sized carrot
1 clove of garlic
1 bay leaf
a blade of mace
1 × 5ml spoon/1 teaspoon lemon juice
1 × 5ml spoon/1 teaspoon anchovy essence
125ml/¼ pint white wine
750ml/1½ pints fish stock (page 12)
salt
1 × 15ml spoon/1 tablespoon cooked lobster coral
50g/2oz butter
25g/1oz flour
125ml/¼ pint single cream
pepper
a few drops red food colouring (optional)

Crush the lobster shell. Flake the rough pieces of flesh finely, keeping the neat pieces for a garnish. Prepare the onion, carrot, and garlic and slice them thinly. Put the shell, flaked lobster, vegetables, bay leaf, mace, lemon juice, anchovy essence, and wine into a deep saucepan. Heat quickly to boiling point and cook briskly for 3–5 minutes. The alcohol in the wine extracts much of the flavour from the lobster and vegetables. Add the fish stock and a little salt. Heat to boiling point, cover, reduce the heat, and simmer for 1 hour.

Strain the soup through a metal sieve and rub through any pieces of firm lobster. Pound the lobster coral with half the butter and rub through a sieve. Melt the rest of the butter in a saucepan and stir in the flour. Gradually add the strained soup and stir until boiling. When at boiling point, whisk in the lobster coral butter. Remove the pan from the heat and stir in the cream. Add salt and pepper to taste. Add the food colouring, if necessary, to obtain a deep orange-pink colour. Add any neat pieces of lobster. Re-heat without boiling the soup.

PRAWN BISQUE

100g/4oz butter
250g/8oz cooked shelled prawns
25g/1oz flour
750ml/1½ pints fish stock (page 12) in which prawn shells have been cooked
125ml/¼ pint white wine
125ml/¼ pint court bouillon (page 12)

1 egg yolk
125ml/¼ pint single cream *or* milk *or* half cream and half milk
salt and pepper
lemon juice
a pinch of grated nutmeg

Melt 25g/1oz of the butter in a saucepan. Add the prawns, and toss over gentle heat for 5 minutes. Pound the prawns, gradually working in another 50g/2oz of the butter. Rub the pounded prawn and butter mixture through a sieve, or process briefly in an electric blender. Melt the remaining 25g/1oz butter in a deep saucepan. Stir in the flour and cook gently for 1–2 minutes. Strain the fish stock and gradually stir it into the flour with the wine and court bouillon. Heat to boiling point. Mix the egg yolk with the cream or milk or both. Season the soup and add lemon juice and nutmeg to taste. Whisk the prawn butter into the soup, at just below boiling point, adding a small pat at a time. Add the egg yolk and cream mixture and stir over low heat, without boiling, to thicken the egg.

THE PRAWN.

BASQUE BEAN SOUP

100g/4oz haricot beans
water
2 medium-sized onions
200g/7oz white cabbage

50g/2oz bacon *or* pork fat
1 clove of garlic
salt and pepper
a few drops white wine vinegar

GARNISH

2 × 15ml spoons/2 tablespoons
   crumbled cooked bacon

Soak the beans in water overnight, then discard the water. Skin
and slice the onions and shred the cabbage. Heat the bacon or pork
fat in a saucepan, add the onions, and fry gently for about 10
minutes until browned. Add the cabbage, and shake the pan over
gentle heat for 2–3 minutes. Skin and crush the garlic and add to
the pan with the soaked beans and 1 litre/2 pints water. Heat the
soup to boiling point and boil briskly for at least 10 minutes.
Cover, and simmer for 1½–2½ hours until the beans are quite soft.
Season and add the vinegar to taste. Just before serving, sprinkle
the bacon on top.

Basque Bean Soup

LENTIL AND PARSLEY SOUP

— *4 helpings* —

2 medium-sized carrots
2 × 15ml spoons/2 tablespoons
  margarine
2 × 15ml spoons/2 tablespoons
  finely chopped leek *or* onion
6 × 15ml spoons/6 tablespoons red
  lentils

500ml/1 pint water
250ml/½ pint milk
salt and pepper
2 × 15ml spoons/2 tablespoons
  chopped parsley
2 × 15ml spoons/2 tablespoons
  chopped Brussels sprouts
  (optional)

Prepare and dice the carrots. Melt the margarine in a saucepan, add the carrots and leek or onion, and fry gently for 2–3 minutes, stirring or tossing frequently. Add the lentils, water, milk, and seasoning. Heat gently to simmering point, cover, and simmer for 30–45 minutes or until the lentils are soft. Re-season if required. Add the chopped parsley, and the sprouts, if used, and serve.

RICE AND TOMATO SOUP

— *4–6 helpings* —

100ml/4fl oz olive oil
200g/7oz long-grain rice
1 clove of garlic
400g/13oz lean bacon
3 medium-sized Spanish onions

4 tomatoes
1 litre/2 pints general household
  stock (page 8)

Heat the oil in a pan, add the rice, and fry until golden-brown. Skin and crush the garlic and stir it into the rice. Chop the bacon into small pieces about 1.25cm/½ inch square. Skin and slice the onions and tomatoes. Fry the bacon gently in a deep saucepan until the fat begins to run. Add the onions and tomatoes, and fry gently until the onion is transparent. Stir in the rice. Add the stock, heat to boiling point, cover, and simmer gently for about 1 hour.

VELVET SOUP

4 helpings

25g/1oz butter
25g/1oz flour
1 × 10ml spoon/1 dessertspoon
   curry powder
500ml/1 pint milk

1 × 15ml spoon/1 tablespoon Patna
   rice
salt and pepper
4 × 10ml spoons/4 dessertspoons
   single cream

Melt the butter in a saucepan, add the flour and curry powder, and fry very gently for 3–5 minutes without hardening the flour. Gradually add the milk, heat to boiling point, and simmer for 5 minutes, stirring all the time.

Meanwhile, cook the rice in boiling water until tender. Drain, and add to the hot soup. Season to taste. Remove the soup from the heat and stir in the cream.

CARAWAY SOUP

6 helpings

50g/2oz bacon *or* pork fat
1 × 10ml spoon/1 dessertspoon
   caraway seeds
50g/2oz flour

a pinch of salt
1 litre/2 pints brown stock (page 6)
salt and pepper

Heat the bacon or pork fat in a deep saucepan, add the caraway seeds, and fry gently for 3–5 minutes. Add the flour and salt, and fry very gently until browned. Add the stock, heat to boiling point, stirring all the time; then simmer gently for 30 minutes. Strain the soup and season to taste.

MINESTRONE

75g/3oz butter beans *or* haricot
  beans
2 rashers streaky bacon, without
  rinds
1 clove of garlic
1 leek
1 onion
2 carrots
50g/2oz French beans
3 sticks celery
2 potatoes

150g/5oz white cabbage
25g/1oz butter
1 bay leaf
1 × 10ml spoon/1 dessertspoon
  concentrated tomato purée
1.25 litres/2½ pints white stock
  (page 9)
salt and pepper
50g/2oz pasta rings

GARNISH

grated Parmesan cheese

Soak the beans overnight in cold water. Drain thoroughly, then
put into fresh water and boil briskly for at least 10 minutes. Drain
thoroughly. Chop the bacon. Skin and crush the garlic. Slice the
leek, onion, carrots, and French beans, chop the celery, dice the
potatoes, and shred the cabbage. Fry the bacon in a saucepan for
2–3 minutes, add the garlic and butter, and fry for 2–3 minutes.
Add all the vegetables and cook for 3–4 minutes. Add the bay leaf,
tomato purée, stock, salt, and pepper. Heat to boiling point,
cover, then simmer for 45–50 minutes. Add the pasta rings and
cook for a further 6–8 minutes.

Serve hot, garnished with grated Parmesan cheese.

VEGETABLE, CHEESE, AND RICE SOUP

6 helpings

¼ cabbage
1 leek
1 large carrot
1 small turnip
1 small onion
50g/2oz butter
25g/1oz long-grain rice

1 × 2.5ml spoon/½ teaspoon sugar
1.25 litres/2½ pints white stock
  (page 9)
salt and pepper
2 × 15ml spoons/2 tablespoons
  grated Cheddar cheese

Shred the cabbage, slice the leek thinly, and dice the carrot, turnip, and onion. Melt the butter in a deep saucepan, add the vegetables and fry gently for 10–15 minutes, without browning them. Add the rice and sugar, and continue cooking, stirring all the time, until all the butter has been absorbed. Stir in the stock and seasoning. Heat to boiling point, cover, and simmer gently for 40 minutes. Sprinkle with grated cheese and serve.

LEEKS.

GARLIC SOUP

(Pistou)

100g/4oz potatoes
2 tomatoes
400g/13oz French beans
4 onions
2 green peppers
200g/7oz vegetable marrow
1½ litres/3 pints water

salt and pepper
50g/2oz vermicelli
3 cloves garlic
1 × 10ml spoon/1 dessertspoon
  olive oil
½ × 2.5ml spoon/¼ teaspoon
  dried basil

Dice the potatoes, and chop the tomatoes, French beans, onions, green peppers, and marrow. Put the water in a saucepan and heat to boiling point; add the vegetables, and simmer for 15–20 minutes. Add the salt, pepper, and vermicelli and cook for a further 8–10 minutes.

Meanwhile, skin and crush the garlic. Pound it with the oil and basil. Add a little hot soup to the garlic and basil, and return the mixture to the saucepan. Stir well and heat through for 2–3 minutes.

Serve with grated Gruyère cheese.

Overleaf
From the back, clockwise
Lentil and Parsley Soup (page 40), Garlic Soup (above) and
Broad Bean and Ham Soup (page 49)

HOLLANDAISE SOUP

6 helpings

1 large carrot
10cm/4 inch piece of cucumber
4 × 10ml spoons/4 tablespoons
  small green peas
white stock (page 9) *or* water
25g/1oz butter *or* margarine
4 × 10ml spoons/4 dessertspoons
  flour

1 litre/2 pints white stock (page 9)
2 egg yolks
75ml/3fl oz milk
50ml/2fl oz single cream
salt and pepper
a sprig of tarragon

Cut pea shapes from the carrot and cucumber to give 4 × 10ml spoons/4 dessertspoons of each. Cook the vegetables in a little boiling stock or water until just tender. Put to one side. Melt the fat in a deep saucepan and stir in the flour. Gradually add the 1 litre/2 pints stock, and stir until boiling. Boil for 2–3 minutes, stirring all the time. Remove from the heat and leave to cool slightly. Mix the egg yolks, milk, and cream in a basin. Pour a little hot soup on to the egg yolk mixture, beating well, then whisk the mixture into the rest of the soup. Stir over gentle heat to thicken the yolks, without boiling the soup. Season to taste. Chop the tarragon and add to the soup with the cooked vegetables; add the cooking liquid also, if liked.

BROAD BEAN AND HAM SOUP

4–6 helpings

625g/1¼lb young shelled
 broad beans
125g/5oz ham *or* bacon in 1 piece
4–5 finely chopped sage leaves
2 small onions
1 × 15ml spoon/1 tablespoon
 chopped parsley

1 × 15ml spoon/1 tablespoon
 concentrated tomato purée
750ml/1½ pints water
4–6 slices brown *or* white bread

Cook the broad beans in boiling salted water until tender; then drain. Meanwhile, cut the ham or bacon into very small pieces, about 6mm/¼ inch square. Skin and chop the onions finely. Heat the ham or bacon gently in a saucepan until the fat begins to run. Add the sage, onions, and parsley, and fry quickly for 2–3 minutes to brown the onion a little.

Add the tomato purée and fry gently for a further 2–3 minutes. Add the water, and heat to boiling point. Add the broad beans to the soup, return to simmering point, partly cover the pan, and simmer for 15 minutes. Toast the slices of bread until golden-brown, and place 1 slice in the bottom of each soup bowl. Pour the hot soup over them, and serve quickly.

BROAD BEAN.

MIDSUMMER SOUP

4–6 helpings

5 small carrots
a bunch of radishes
1 small cauliflower
100g/4oz mange-tout peas
1.5 litres/3 pints water
50g/2oz shelled green peas

4 × 15ml spoons/4 tablespoons
 flour
1 × 5ml spoon/1 teaspoon meat
 extract
salt and pepper
1 egg yolk
100ml/4fl oz single cream

Slice the carrots and radishes, break the cauliflower into florets, and top and tail the mange-tout peas. Heat the water to boiling point in a large saucepan. Add all the vegetables and simmer until tender. Blend the flour with a little cold water and stir it into the soup. Simmer gently for another 5 minutes to thicken the soup. Add the meat extract and seasoning to taste. Mix together the yolk and cream. Pour a little hot soup on to the mixture and stir until blended. Add the mixture to the rest of the soup and heat gently, without boiling, to thicken the yolk.

Serve hot with cheese biscuits.

Midsummer Soup

VEGETABLE SOUP

500g/1lb vegetables (approx)
15–25g/½–1oz butter, margarine *or* other fat
500ml–1 litre/1–2 pints white stock (page 9) *or* general household stock (page 8)
bouquet garni *or* flavouring herbs
lemon juice

salt and pepper
125ml/¼ pint milk
2 × 10ml spoons/2 dessertspoons thickening (flour, cornflour, ground rice, tapioca, *or* potato) for each 500ml/1 pint puréed soup
cold stock, water *or* milk

FOR CREAM OF VEGETABLE SOUP

add
4–8 × 15ml spoons/4–8 tablespoons single cream and/or
1 egg yolk

Prepare and chop the vegetables. Melt the fat in a deep saucepan, add the vegetables, and fry gently for 5–10 minutes without browning them. Add the stock, bouquet garni or herbs, lemon juice, and seasoning to taste. Heat to boiling point, reduce the heat, and simmer gently until the vegetables are quite soft. Do not overcook.

Remove the bouquet garni. Purée the vegetables and liquid by either rubbing through a fine sieve, or by processing in an electric blender. Add the milk, measure the soup, and return it to a clean pan. Weigh the thickening in the correct proportion and blend it with a little cold stock, water or milk. Stir it into the soup. Bring to the boil, stirring all the time, and cook for 5 minutes. Re-season if required.

Serve with croûtons or Melba toast.

Note To make a cream of vegetable soup, remove the pan from the heat after the soup has been thickened and leave to cool slightly. Add a little of the hot soup to the single cream (which can replace some of the milk in the main recipe) and egg yolk, if using, and beat well. Whisk the mixture into the rest of the soup. Return the soup to gentle heat and re-heat, without boiling, stirring all the time.

SWEETCORN SOUP

4 helpings

3 young sweetcorn cobs *or* 375g/
    12oz canned sweetcorn kernels
    (approx)
1 × 10ml spoon/1 dessertspoon
    butter

500ml/1 pint white stock (page 9)
salt and pepper
a pinch of grated nutmeg

Remove the husks, silks, and tassels from the fresh cobs, and cut off the kernels. Melt the butter in a deep saucepan, add the kernels and scraped cobs, and fry gently for 10 minutes. Add the stock, heat to boiling point, reduce the heat, cover, and simmer gently for 1–1½ hours or until the kernels are quite soft. Remove the scraped cobs and reserve 2 × 15ml spoons/2 tablespoons kernels for the garnish. Rub the rest of the kernels and the liquid through a sieve. Add salt, pepper, and nutmeg to taste. Re-heat the soup to boiling point. Add the reserved kernels.

PIMENTO SOUP

4–6 helpings

3–4 sweet red peppers
1 medium-sized onion
1–2 tomatoes
1 litre/2 pints white stock (page 9)
salt
Cayenne pepper

2 × 10ml spoons/2 dessertspoons
    cornflour for each 500ml/1 pint
    puréed soup
cold stock *or* water
sugar

Prepare and slice the vegetables. Put the stock in a deep saucepan and heat to boiling point. Add the vegetables and simmer until soft. Rub the soup through a fine sieve, measure it, and return to the pan. Season to taste. Blend the required amount of cornflour with a little cold stock or water. Stir the cornflour paste into the soup and re-heat until the cornflour has thickened. Add sugar to taste.

COUNTRY SOUP

625g/1¼lb mixed vegetables
(carrot, turnip, onion, leek,
celery, tomato)
2 × 15ml spoons/2 tablespoons
bacon fat

500ml/1 pint white stock (page 9),
water *or* water in which
vegetables have been cooked
25g/1oz brown bread
250ml/½ pint milk
salt and pepper

GARNISH

chopped parsley *or* other fresh
herbs

Grate the carrot and turnip coarsely, and chop the onion, leek, celery, and tomato. Melt the bacon fat in a deep saucepan, add all the vegetables except the tomato, and fry gently until they begin to brown. Add the stock or water and the tomato. Toast the brown bread, break it up roughly, and add it to the soup. Heat to boiling point, cover, and simmer for 45 minutes or until the vegetables are quite soft. Rub the soup through a fine sieve. Stir in the milk, and season to taste. Re-heat before serving. Garnish each portion with chopped herbs.

Serve with bread croûtons.

COLD SOUPS

CHILLED PEA SOUP WITH YOGHURT

—— *4 helpings* ——

150g/5oz potatoes
1 medium-sized onion
3–4 lettuce leaves
250g/8oz frozen green peas

500ml/1 pint chicken stock (page 10)
275g/9oz natural yoghurt
salt and pepper
a pinch of sugar

Peel and slice the potatoes and onion, and shred the lettuce leaves. Put with most of the peas into a saucepan with the stock and heat to boiling point. Reduce the heat and simmer for 10 minutes. Rub the soup through a fine sieve, or process in an electric blender. Whisk the yoghurt until the curd is evenly broken down, and add to the soup, reserving 4 × 15ml spoonfuls/4 tablespoons as a garnish. Chill for several hours. Add salt, pepper, and a little sugar to taste. Serve garnished with the remaining peas and yoghurt.

CUCUMBER AND YOGHURT SOUP

4 helpings

1 small onion
½ cucumber
1 × 15ml spoon/1 tablespoon
    butter
400g/13oz natural yoghurt
250ml/½ pint chicken stock (page
    10)

grated rind and juice of ½ lemon
½ × 15ml spoon/½ tablespoon
    finely chopped mint
salt and pepper

GARNISH

sprigs of mint

Skin and chop the onion finely. Peel the cucumber and cut the flesh into 6mm/¼ inch dice. Melt the butter in a saucepan and cook the onion and cucumber gently, without browning them, for 8–10 minutes. Leave to cool. Whisk the yoghurt until the curd is evenly broken down and add to the soup with the stock. Add the lemon rind and juice, and mint. Season to taste. Chill for several hours. Serve garnished with sprigs of mint.

THE CUCUMBER.

SUMMER SOUP WITH BUTTERMILK

4 helpings

½ green pepper
½ cucumber
250ml/½ pint buttermilk

250ml/½ pint tomato juice
grated rind and juice of ½ lemon
salt and pepper

GARNISH

chopped parsley

Prepare and dice the vegetables. Put the green pepper into a saucepan with a little cold water and heat to boiling point. Drain, and leave to cool. Mix together the buttermilk and tomato juice and add the pepper, cucumber, lemon rind and juice. Season with salt and pepper. Chill for several hours. Serve sprinkled with the chopped parsley.

Summer Soup with Buttermilk

JELLIED TOMATO SOUP WITH SOURED CREAM

4 helpings

400g/13oz piece honeydew melon (optional)
250ml/½ pint chicken stock (page 10)
2 spring onions
2–3 celery leaves
250ml/½ pint tomato juice
a few drops Worcestershire sauce
3 cloves
a pinch of sugar
a few drops lemon juice
salt
Cayenne pepper
1 × 15ml spoon/1 tablespoon gelatine
2 × 15ml spoons/2 tablespoons water

GARNISH

4 × 10ml spoons/4 dessertspoons soured cream
freshly ground black pepper

Remove the seeds from the melon, if using, and scoop out the flesh with a ball scoop. Chill the melon balls and the chicken stock while preparing the other ingredients.

Chop the onions finely and shred the celery leaves. Put into a large saucepan with the tomato juice, Worcestershire sauce, cloves, sugar, and lemon juice. Season to taste, half cover, and simmer for 10 minute. Remove from the heat and strain into a bowl.

Soften the gelatine in the water in a small heat-proof basin. Stand the basin in a pan of hot water and stir until it has dissolved. Add a little of the strained tomato liquid and stir well. Pour the gelatine into the rest of the tomato liquid and mix well. Add the chilled chicken stock, stir until well blended, and leave to set.

To serve, whisk the jellied soup until frothy. Spoon into 4 chilled bowls, and gently mix in the melon balls, if using. Garnish with soured cream and the black pepper.

CHICKEN AND BEETROOT BROTH

6 helpings

400g/13oz young uncooked
   beetroots
1 litre/2 pints water
400g/13oz cooked chicken *or* veal
200g/7oz cooked ham
2–3 lettuce hearts
2 long *or* 5 small cucumbers

6 hard-boiled eggs
salt and pepper
a little made English mustard
250ml/½ pint soured cream
1 × 15ml spoon/1 tablespoon
   chopped fennel leaves *or* stem
6 ice cubes

GARNISH

2 × 15ml spoons/2 tablespoons
   chopped green part of spring
   onion *or* chives

Wash and peel the beetroots. Heat the water to boiling point, add the beetroots, cover, and simmer gently for 1 hour. Strain off the liquid and leave to cool. Chop the chicken or veal, the ham, and lettuce hearts into small pieces. Peel and dice the cucumbers. Separate the hard-boiled egg yolks from the whites and sieve the yolks into a bowl. Add salt, pepper, and the mustard to the yolks and gradually stir in the soured cream. Add the chicken, ham, lettuce, and cucumbers, and stir well. Pour the cold beetroot juice over them, and mix well. Chill in a refrigerator for 2–3 hours.

Just before serving, chop the egg white and add it to the soup with the fennel. Put an ice cube in each bowl and pour the soup over it.

Serve with the chopped spring onion tops or chives.

Note The beetroots can be puréed and added to the liquid if liked, to make a very thick soup.

CHILLED AVOCADO SOUP

4 ripe avocado pears
juice of 1 lemon
500ml/1 pint consommé (page 21)
   or canned consommé

250ml/½ pint soured cream
salt and pepper

GARNISH

chopped chives *or* green part of
   spring onions

Scoop out the flesh from the avocado pears, and mix with the lemon juice. Rub through a sieve. Mix the avocado, consommé, and soured cream until blended, and season to taste. Chill in a refrigerator for 2–3 hours. Just before serving, add the chives or spring onions.

THE LEMON.